CANALS

BY CASS R. SANDAK

An Easy-Read Modern Wonders Book

FRANKLIN WATTS

New York/London/Toronto/Sydney

1983

Over: a large boat carries ore through the St. Lambert Lock on the St. Lawrence Seaway.

FOR NORA

R.L. 3.5 Spache Revised Formula

Cover photograph courtesy of Panama Canal Commission.

Photographs courtesy of: St. Lawrence Seaway Authority: pp. 1, 14 (top), 26 (right); Michigan Travel Bureau: pp. 4, 26 (left); Illinois Department of Commerce and Community Affairs: p. 6 (top); Consulate General of the Netherlands: pp. 6 (bottom right), 20 (right); German Information Center: pp. 8 (left), 20 (left); Army Corps of Engineers: pp. 8 (right), 9 (left and right), 11, 12 (top and bottom); Panama Canal Commission: pp. 13 (top), 15, 25; Ewing Galloway: p. 13 (bottom); Bettman Archive: pp. 17, 18; Sovfoto/Eastfoto: p. 19; French Embassy Press and Information Division: p. 21 (left); British Tourist Authority: p. 21 (right); Canal Museum, Syracuse, N.Y.: pp. 22, 23; Fred J. Maroon: p. 28; Smithsonian Institution: p. 14 (bottom); the author: pp. 6 (bottom left).

The author wishes to thank Mr. Tiffany Bailey for his help.

Diagrams by Jane Kendall

Library of Congress Cataloging in Publication Data

Sandak, Cass R.
  Canals.

  (An Easy-read modern wonders book)
  Includes index.
  Summary: Describes how canals are built, their uses, and how they might be designed and used in the future. Also discusses such famous canals as the Suez Canal, the Panama Canal, the Erie Canal, and the St. Lawrence Seaway.
        1. Canals—Juvenile literature. [1. Canals]
  I. Title. II. Series.
  TC745.S25 1983   627'.13   83-12396
  ISBN 0-531-04625-7

Contents

About Canals

Canals are waterways made by people. Sometimes they are formed from rivers or bodies of water that are already there. But usually they are dug out of the land. Many canals cut across land to connect two bodies of water.

Canals are of different sizes and have different uses. Some canals carry water to dry farmland. These are called **irrigation canals**. Other canals drain marshy areas or carry water away. They are known as **drainage canals**.

Many canals help make transportation easier. They are known as **transportation canals**. These canals are used for navigation by barges, boats, and ships.

Some canals can shorten a sea journey. The Suez Canal and the Panama Canal save ships many thousands of miles of travel.

Canals can turn inland cities into ports. Sometimes cities that are many miles from the sea become important shipping centers. Canals join these cities to the sea or to rivers or lakes that go to the sea. In the United States, the cities of Chicago, Cleveland, Houston, and Seattle are such ports. Manchester, England, and Liege,

One of the world's busiest navigation canals, the Sault Sainte Marie (or "Soo") Canal bypasses rapids. The locks allow ships to go into Lake Superior.

Because of canals in the St. Lawrence Seaway, large cargo ships can sail to an inland city like Chicago.

Belgium, are other examples of port cities that are not on the sea.

Some cities have so many canals that the waterways are really like streets! Venice, in Italy, is famous for its canals. There boats often take the place of automobiles and buses. Amsterdam, in the Netherlands, is often called the "Venice of the North," because it has so many canals.

Left, Venice, and *right*, Amsterdam. Both of these European cities are famous for their canals.

What Are Canals Like?

A canal is a large ditch that is usually widest at the top. The bottom, or **bed,** of the canal is narrower. The sides or walls of a canal slope down so they are less likely to cave in.

The **landline** is the distance along which a canal can be built on one level. When the land is not level, a canal must be built at different levels. **Locks** are needed to connect the sections of a canal. They allow boats to pass from one level of the canal to another.

Reaches are stretches of level land or the sections of a canal between locks. Even the reaches of a level canal are sometimes divided by **stop gates** or **safety gates.** These can close off a section of the canal if repairs are needed.

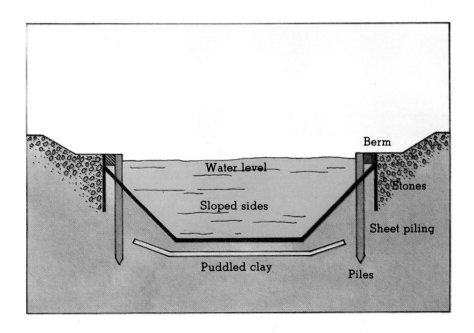

Generally, the smallest canals are used for irrigation and drainage. Larger canals are used for navigation. There are two kinds of navigation canals: barge canals and ship canals.

The main difference between a barge canal and a ship canal is size. Barge canals are narrow and shallow. Because of this, only barges—small, flat-bottomed cargo boats—and other small craft can use them. Ship canals are large enough to carry oceangoing vessels.

Left: barge traffic on the Mittelland Canal, near Hanover, Germany. *Right:* the Cape Cod Canal, a ship canal in Massachusetts.

Sometimes canals are not dug. They are formed out of existing rivers or waterways. **Lateral canals** run along the side of a river or very close to a river. They bypass rapids or waterfalls in the main river. There are many lateral canals in Canada that form passages in the St. Lawrence Seaway system.

Sometimes small or shallow rivers with many currents, rocks, rapids, or falls are made into canals. When this happens, they are said to be **canalized.** Small dams, called **weirs,** may raise the water enough to allow navigation.

Left: a modern irrigation canal in Tennessee. *Right:* canals often run parallel to other bodies of water that are not easily navigated.

Building a Canal

When a canal is built, large amounts of earth and rock must be dug away. Thousands of workers with picks and shovels built the first canals. When the Erie Canal was built, horse-drawn plows helped with the work. Today bulldozers, tractors, steam shovels, and dump trucks make canal building faster and easier.

Engineers who design modern canals must follow the principles of **hydraulics**. This is the science of water and waterways.

Engineers must plan the best route for the canal. They must find out how deep and how wide a canal should be. There must be enough space under, around, and over vessels that pass through a canal. This space is called **clearance**. If boats that pass through a canal are large and the canal is small, the banks will wear away quickly.

This wearing away, or **erosion**, is worst near the top, or **waterline**, of the canal. A **berm** is a narrow shelf scooped out near the waterline of a canal ditch. Vessels passing through the canal create **wash**, small waves that can wear away the sides. The berm helps keep the banks from eroding.

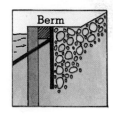

Berm

Where a canal passes through soft earth, sand, or marshy areas, the sides may crumble and the canal bed may fill up with earth. Upright wooden posts called **piles** or stone walls keep the sides from falling in. Modern builders sometimes line the sides and bottoms of canals with concrete. Often the banks are protected at the waterline with stone rubble, or **pitching**.

Canals dug through soft dirt or sand have to be cleaned out, or **dredged**. Sand and silt must be pumped up from the bottom and put on the banks. If there is too much sand in the canal bed, ships may not be able to pass through.

Keeping the water in a canal presents problems. Water sinks into the ground and the sides. The bed and sides of a canal are lined, often with

A canal under construction in Tennessee

puddled clay. This is a mixture of sand and clay. It makes a watertight lining around the bed and sides. This prevents leakage and keeps the canal full.

Water from rivers, streams, lakes, and reservoirs is used to keep the water level in a canal high enough. Modern canals often have underground pipes that carry water in from these places.

If there is too much water in a canal, this water is carried away by **waste-weirs,** or drainage canals. A drainage canal must slope enough to carry water away from the site.

Canal designers must overcome natural obstacles. Workers may have to blast through rock with powerful explosives. Where a canal passes through a low-lying area, **embankments,** or banks, may have to be built up along the sides.

Concrete
reinforcement is
often used when a
modern canal is
being built.

12

The Gaillard Cut in
the Panama Canal

Sometimes a mountain blocks a canal route.
Then it may be easier to cut through it than to
build a system of locks to pass over it. **Cuts** are
excavations open to the sky that let a canal pass
through a mountain. They are made by blasting
and digging through rock and soil. The Gaillard
Cut is 8 miles (12.8 km) long. It is one of the most
famous parts of the Panama Canal.

Much of the
Corinth Canal in
Greece cuts through
tall layers of
rock. The deepest
cut is 285 feet
(85.5 m).

Sometimes canals cross over tunnels. Here Canada's Welland Ship Canal is above a road and railroad tunnel.

Tunnels are another way to let a canal pass through a mountain. The Rove Canal in France has a tunnel that is 4½ miles (7.2 km) long. But it is 72 feet (21.9 m) across—one of the largest tunnel openings in the world.

A canal may have to be carried across a valley, or other low-lying area. Sometimes an **aqueduct** is used to do this. An aqueduct is like a trough supported on pillars. Sometimes an aqueduct passes right over another body of water.

An aqueduct carries a canal over a river. This old photograph shows the Lackawaxen Aqueduct in Pennsylvania.

Locks

Locks make it possible for canals to climb over hills. Locks may also be built where there is a waterfall. A group of locks can make a "stairway" that ships can climb up or down.

A lock is built where different water levels in a canal meet. A lock is a section of the canal that is walled off to form a rectangular box. Watertight gates open at both ends of the lock. The level of the water inside the lock can be raised or lowered to match the water level outside the lock at either end.

A view of the Pedro Miguel Locks in the Panama Canal. The ship on the right is about to sail into the empty lock; the ship in the distance on the left has been raised and will soon sail on.

(1)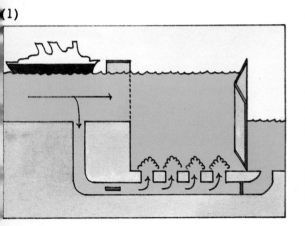

(2)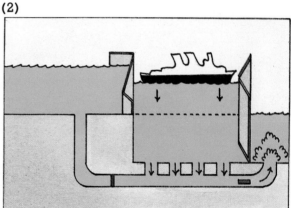

If a boat goes into the lock from the lower level, the gate at the end is closed behind it. Water is pumped in to fill the lock. As the water level in the lock rises, the boat rises with it. When the water level inside the lock is the same as the water level outside of the higher end, the lock is filled. Then the gates at the higher end are opened and the boat continues on its journey.

Before locks were invented, around A.D. 1000, canals could only be built where the land was level. Because water runs downhill, the water would flow out of a canal that was built on a slope. Sometimes, however, two separate canals on different levels were built. Then boats had to be dragged overland between the canals.

By 1400 locks were already in use in Europe. In early times the gates of a lock had to be opened and closed by hand. Later, locks were equipped

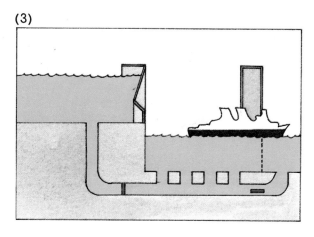

(3)

A ship goes through a lock. (1) The ship is about to enter a filled lock that is level with the water behind it. (2) The water is taken out of the lock and the ship is lowered to the level of the next stretch of the canal. (3) The ship can now proceed on its journey.

with wheels and gears that could be powered by people or animals. Finally, electric lock gates were invented.

Most modern locks are built of concrete. Some have walls covered with steel. Some have sides supported by wood pilings and a floor of rock or sand.

The giant Eisenhower Lock of the St. Lawrence Seaway under construction. Because locks are expensive to build and operate, engineers plan canals that require as few as possible.

17

A battleship enters the Gatun Locks in the Panama Canal. The V shape of the miter gate is shown in the foreground.

Water pours in and out through large pipes, or **culverts.** The ends of the locks are fitted with **sluice gates** or **miter gates.** A sluice gate is a single piece of steel that can be raised, lowered, or rolled across the entrance. Miter gates have two sections that swing in an arch, or **V.** The point of the **V** heads into the higher water. The weight of the water actually helps to open and close the miter gates. Leonardo da Vinci invented the miter gate lock in 1480 and it is still the type most widely used.

The difference in level between two sections, or reaches, of a canal is called the **lift.** A few locks raise ships more than 100 feet (30 m). But most locks only raise or lower ships 20 to 40 feet (6 to 12 m).

Inclined planes are another way to move ships between levels of a canal. They are smooth surfaces sometimes paved with rounded stones or rollers.

Canals Through the Ages

Early Canals

The first canals were used mainly for irrigation in parts of the world where water is scarce. Many of these canals were in ancient Egypt and the Middle East. Remains of the oldest known canal are in Iraq and date from 5000 B.C. Three thousand years ago, in Babylon, King Nebuchadnezzar had the Tigris and Euphrates rivers joined by a canal.

The Canals of Europe

The ancient Romans built canals near their settlements in Italy, France, and England. Today the continent of Europe is crisscrossed with an elaborate river and canal system. Some of the canals are hundreds of years old. Around the year 800, the Holy Roman Emperor Charlemagne dreamed of a canal system that would allow ships to sail from the North Sea all the way to the ports of the Black Sea.

The Grand Canal of China was completed around 1300. Today, at more than 1,060 miles (1,700 km), it is still the world's longest canal.

Today a series of five canal systems that were built between the 1780s and 1968 link the Rhine, Main, and Danube rivers. Boats and barges can sail all but 39 miles (62.7 km) of the 2,100-mile (3,380-km) route from the North Sea to the Black Sea. The German government hopes to complete the last section in the near future.

Since 1250, the people of the Netherlands have used canals for drainage in their low-lying country. They now have more than 4,240 miles (6,823 km) of canals that connect Dutch cities.

The Languedoc Canal is sometimes called the first modern canal system. It connects the Mediterranean Sea with the Bay of Biscay, on the Atlantic Ocean. The canal has over a hundred locks. The canal was completed in 1681 and saves French ships a voyage of over 1,000 miles (1,600 km) through the Straits of Gibraltar and around Spain.

Before railroads were invented in the early nineteenth century, overland travel was slow and

Left: a barge passes under a bridge on a stretch of Germany's canal system. *Right:* Volkerak Lock. On some days, more than 700 ships pass through this Dutch lock.

difficult. People who wanted to go a long distance had to ride horses or travel in uncomfortable coaches or wagons. Canals helped make travel by water easier and cheaper. In the seventeenth and eighteenth centuries, many hundreds of miles of canals were built between European cities.

Canals in the United States

George Washington and the founding fathers of the United States thought that canals could join American settlements. The first canal in the United States was finished in 1796 in South Hadley, Massachusetts.

By 1850, many eastern cities and some midwestern cities were connected by a canal system. Agricultural products, raw materials, and manufactured goods were carried between cities of the developing nation on canals. In this way, canals helped shape the early growth of the United States.

Left: the Languedoc Canal extends 148 miles (238 km) across southern France. *Right:* canal cruising in Scotland. Many European canals are used for recreation.

The Erie Canal

Thousands of workers labored for many years to complete the Erie Canal. Workers had to clear a 60-foot (18-m) wide path through forests and marshlands. Trees were cut down and bridges were built across the canal.

The Erie Canal was built in three main parts, beginning in 1817. It was finally completed in 1825. In 1835 it was enlarged and improved. It provided cheap and easy transport and helped to open trade to the western part of the country.

The canal was 360 miles (579 km) long and connected the Hudson River with Lake Erie. It ran from Albany to Buffalo across most of New York State. The canal was 40 feet (12 m) wide at the waterline and 12 feet (3.6 m) deep. The walls of the canal were lined with wooden piles and sloped down to a width of 28 feet (8.5 m) at the bottom.

A series of stepped locks at Lockport, New York. The photo was taken about 1880.

22

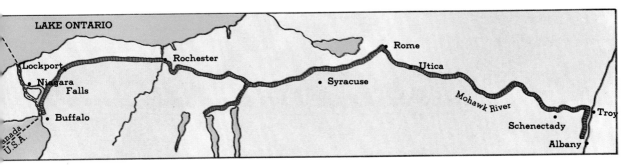

A series of locks helped boats get from one end of the canal to the other. The locks were made of stone set in cement. The lock gates were made of wood.

Mules walked along **towpaths** that were raised 4 feet (1.2 m) above the level of the canal. Long, narrow **packet boats** carried passengers up and down the canal. Some boats were homes for **canalers** who made their living carrying freight and passengers along the canal.

The success of the Erie Canal inspired more canal building in the United States and around the world. Although most of the Erie Canal is no longer used, some portions of it were used in making the New York State Barge Canal.

Mules hauled boats and barges through the canal at about 4 miles (6.4 km) an hour.

The Panama Canal

The Panama Canal joins the Atlantic Ocean and the Pacific Ocean. If it were not for this canal, ships would have to go the entire way around South America.

For a long time, the United States wanted to build a canal that would cut through the Isthmus of Panama. They finally built the Panama Canal over a ten-year period, from 1904 to 1914. Using steam shovels, workers dug away more than 240 million cubic yards (184 million cu m) of earth and rock to build the canal. Swamps and breeding places for mosquitoes carrying yellow fever and malaria had to be drained.

The Panama Canal is about 51 miles (82 km) long. It runs in a southeastern direction from the entrance on the Atlantic side to the mouth of the

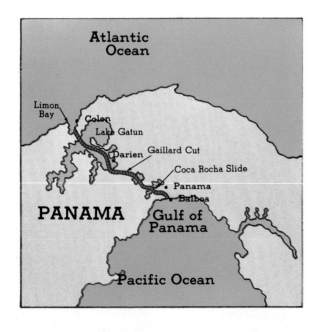

canal on the Pacific end. The canal shortens the sailing route by more than 7,800 miles (12,552 km).

Powerful train locomotives pull ships through the locks in the Panama Canal.

The shallowest part of the canal is only 41 feet (12.4 m) deep. The channel is wide enough to allow two small ships to pass, but the largest ships cannot fit through the waterway. Plans to make the canal wider and deeper are being talked about.

The sea levels at each end of the canal are very different. Twelve locks set in pairs allow ships to pass through. Panama Canal locks are 1,000 feet long (305 m), 110 feet (33 m) wide, and 70 feet (21 m) deep. It takes a ship about seven to eight hours to make the trip through the canal.

The St. Lawrence Seaway

The St. Lawrence Seaway is made up of the St. Lawrence River and a series of canals, dams, and locks. These make an international waterway shared by Canada and the United States.

Together with the Great Lakes, the seaway forms a 2,342-mile (3,769-km) waterway system. The seaway joins the Atlantic Ocean with the western end of Lake Superior in the heart of North America.

The St. Lawrence Seaway has three main stretches of canals. The canal sections are 27 feet

Left: an aerial view of the Sault Sainte Marie Canal and locks. *Right:* Beauharnois Lock. The seaway is free of ice from April to December.

(8.2 m) deep. The St. Lawrence river has been fitted with seven locks that connect Montreal with Lake Ontario. These seven locks are 766 feet (233.5 m) long and 80 feet (24.3 m) wide. This is the newest part. It was opened in 1959.

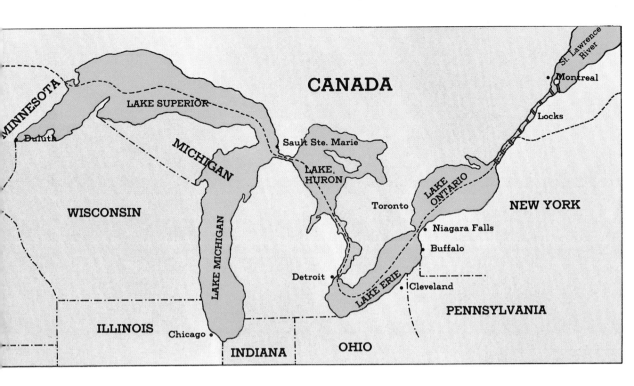

The Welland Ship Canal in southeast Ontario, Canada, is 27.6 miles (44 km) long. It connects Lake Ontario with Lake Erie and bypasses Niagara Falls. Eight locks overcome the 326-foot (99.3-m) difference in lake levels.

The Sault (pronounced Soo) Sainte Marie, or Soo, Canal, is one of the world's busiest canals. *Sault* is the French word for rapids. These rapids are between Lake Huron and Lake Superior. There are actually two Soo canals, built in 1855 and in 1895.

Iron, steel, grain, and manufactured goods are the most popular cargoes. Hydroelectric facilities along the seaway provide power to communities in Canada and the United States.

Since the Suez Canal is all on one level, it has no locks.

The Suez Canal

The Suez Canal links Europe and the Mediterranean Sea with the Indian Ocean. The canal cuts across the Isthmus of Suez, which connects Egypt and the Sinai Peninsula. By going through the Suez Canal, ships do not have to travel around the continent of Africa.

The Suez Canal is more than 100 miles (160.9 km) long, 500 feet (150 m) wide at the waterline, and 36 feet (10.9 m) deep. At the bottom, the Suez is 196 feet (59.7 m) wide. The canal is deep enough so that most ships can travel through it. It takes a ship about fifteen hours to pass through the canal.

The modern Suez Canal replaced an older one that was built around 2000 B.C. The new canal took ten years to build, from 1859 to 1869. It was planned and constructed by a French engineer, Ferdinand de Lesseps.

28

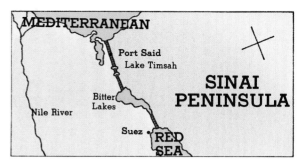

The Suez is one of the world's most famous canals. Traffic through the canal has been interrupted during the recent wars in the Middle East.

Canals Today and Tomorrow

Industry needs raw materials like coal, oil, and steel. Canal shipping is still cheaper than train or motor transport.

In the future many new canals will be built to supply water to dry lands. The world's largest irrigation canal is now being built in Turkey. And canals with swift currents, like the Moscow-Volga Canal, make electricity to supply energy needs.

Canals are as useful today as they ever have been. Modern equipment and knowledge make canal building easier. They help engineers and designers overcome problems in building new canals or enlarging old ones.

Words About Canals

Aqueduct. A structure that carries a canal over a river or a valley.

Bed. The bottom of a canal.

Berm. A ledge near the waterline of a canal. It helps keep the bank of the canal from washing away.

Canaler. A person who lives or works on a canal boat.

Canalized. When a body of water is made into a canal, it is canalized.

Clearance. The space between a boat and the sides and bottom of a canal.

Culvert. A large pipe through which water passes to fill a lock.

Cut. An open excavation that lets a canal pass through a mountain.

Drainage canals. Canals that carry water away from a place.

Embankments. A bank that is built up along the sides of a canal.

Erosion. The wearing away of the banks of a canal.

Hydraulics. The science of water and waterways.

Irrigation canal. A canal that brings water to dry places.

Isthmus. A narrow strip of land that connects two larger pieces of land.

Landline. The distance along which a canal can be built all on one level.

Lateral canals. Canals that run alongside, or near, a river.

Lift. The difference in level between two sections of a canal.

Miter gate. A gate on a lock which swings open in an arch, or **V**.

Packet boat. A small boat that carries cargo on a barge canal.

Piles. Upright wooden posts that support the sides of a canal.

Pitching. Stone pieces that are used to protect canal banks.

Puddled clay. A mixture of sand and clay, used to line the bed and sides of a canal.

Reaches. Stretches of level land on a canal. They are also the sections of a canal between locks.

Safety gate. A gate that can close off a section of a canal if repairs are needed. Also known as a stop gate.

Sluice gate. A gate made from a single piece of steel at the end of a lock.

Towpath. A path alongside a canal. People and animals walk along this path and guide the boats through.

Transportation canal. A canal used for navigation by barges, boats, and ships.

Wash. Small waves created by vessels passing through a canal. Wash can wear away, or erode, canal sides.

Waterline. The surface level of the water in a canal.

Weir. Small dams that raise the water level enough so that ships may pass through.

Index